MIKOLAJEWSKA · DESIRE

Desire
Came upon that One
in the Beginning …

Creation Hymns of the Rig Veda

Barbara Mikolajewska

The Lintons' Video Press
New Haven
2017

Publication history: first edition, © 1997,
published under ISBN-10: 0-9659529-0-8
by The Lintons' Video Press, New Haven, CT;
previewed in the *Journal of the Society for
Indian Philosophy and Religion*, 1997;
second edition, revised and enlarged, © 1999,
published under ISBN-10: 0-9659529-1-6
in various printings, 1999 - 2009.

ISBN-10: 0-9659529-1-6
ISBN-13: 978-0-9659529-1-0

Contents

Acknowledgments

All extracts from the *Rig Veda* appearing in what follows come from the Penguin Classics edition, in the translation of Wendy Doniger O'Flaherty: *The Rig Veda: An Anthology*, Penguin Books, London, 1981 (ISBN: 0-14-044402-5), and have been reproduced with the generous permission of Professor Doniger.

Similarly, all reference to the writings of René Girard focuses on his volumes *A Theater of Envy* (Oxford University Press, New York, 1991), *Things Hidden since the Foundation of the World* (Stanford University Press, Stanford, 1987), and *The Scapegoat* (The Johns Hopkins University Press, Baltimore, 1989).

Finally, thanks are due to Professors Chandana and Kisor Chakrabarti, at whose kind invitation a preliminary version of this work was presented to the Society for Indian Philosophy and Religion at its Conference on Relativism held in Calcutta in August of 1997.

Introduction

It can sometimes be enlightening to examine one worldview from the perspective of another. In exactly such a spirit, but without taking sides, what follows is an attempt at rereading the *Creation Hymns* of the *Rig Veda* from the mimetic perspective espoused by René Girard. Whatever actual enlightenment the reader may inadvertently find in these pages is, of course, purely coincidental.

Girard's approach to religious texts is that of a Realist. Religious texts, he claims, make statements about the reality of social impasses that arise from the human predicament. Indeed, they develop as direct outgrowths of that reality. They themselves, in turn, foster another social reality by providing a religious prescription against these impasses.

Religious texts ultimately refer to *mimesis*, which is the ancient Greek word for imitation and for creation of images, and to the *mimetic crisis*. They also have their beginnings in mimesis; and they try to find a remedy against it. Religious narratives are hidden sources of knowledge about the paradoxes of mimesis seen as the force that creates and destroys the human universe.

Mimesis, as inherent in the process of Desire (*conflictual* mimesis), destroys the universe by that very process. It implants conflict into human interactions. Mimesis creates a new universe when it shifts from *conflictual* to *imperative*, to the mimesis that provokes harmonious compliance with normative demands of society (*imperative* mimesis). Thus mimesis destroys the universe by the process of desire, and it creates a new universe when it shifts from the *conflictual* to the *imperative*: a successful shifting is the new creation. This shifting of mimesis is accomplished by means of what Girard calls *victimage*: the mimetic production of divinity and of sacrifice. How exactly are these produced? They are mimetic copies of the *founding murder*. The concept of the founding murder refers to a hypothetical violent event (*scapegoating*) that brings to an end the destruction characteristic of the mimetic crisis brought on by the process of desire.

To create the new universe means to shift from conflictual to imperative mimesis. Who, or what, can accomplish such a radical change? Religions say: this is the work of the Creator and of sacrifice. Girard says: this is done by mimesis. The Creation Hymns of the *Rig Veda* provide both answers at once.

Chapter I

Desire Came upon that One in the Beginning...

Desire and the Beginning of the World

Desire came upon that one in the beginning;
that was the first seed of mind.
Poets seeking in their heart with wisdom
found the bond of existence in non-existence.

The *Rig Veda: Creation Hymn* (*Nāsadīya*), 10.129, 4

11

The Creation Hymn *Nāsadīya* of the *Rig Veda* connects the creation of the universe with desire. The connection, however, remains for this Hymn a mystery, as does the creation of the universe itself. René Girard's concept of mimetic desire provides some answers to the questions this Hymn asks.

1. On violent undifferentiation

The hymn *Nāsadīya,* the 10.129th Hymn of the *Rig Veda*, makes three somehow surprising statements:

1. It connects the creation of the universe with desire: (4) *Desire came upon that one in the beginning; ... .*

2. It separates creation from the gods and distinguishes it from the creation of the universe:

(6) *Whence is this creation? The gods came afterwards, with the creation of this universe. Who then knows whence it has arisen?*

(7) *Whence this creation has arisen — perhaps it formed itself, or perhaps it did not ...*

3. It sees the life force as emerging from the cosmic no-thing-ness (the Void) that was in the beginning. This Void will stand as the Vedic counterpart of the violent undifferentiation of the Girardian mimetic crisis.

Everything was undifferentiated in the beginning. There were no oppositions, no differences:

(1) *There was neither non-existence nor existence then; there was neither the realm of space nor the sky which is beyond. ...*

(2) *There was neither death nor immortality then. There was no distinguishing sign of night nor of day.*

(3) *Darkness was hidden by darkness in the beginning; with no distinguishing sign, all this was water.*

However, there was something in the beginning. There was some action, something got generated:

(1) *What stirred? Where? In whose protection? ...*

(2) *That one breathed, windless, by its own impulse. Other than that there was nothing beyond.*

(3) *The life force that was covered with emptiness ... arose through the power of heat.*

Differences were born from that power of heat, which means contemplation of the divine, and renunciation of desires: a kind of asceticism dedicated to the gods. We learn about the power of heat in detail from the 10.190[th] Hymn of the *Rig Veda*.

(1) *Order and truth were born from heat as it blazed up. From that was born night; from that heat was born the billowy ocean.*

(2) *From the billowy ocean was born the year, that arranges days and nights, ruling over all that blinks its eyes.*

(3) *The Arranger has set in their proper place the sun and moon, the sky and the earth, the middle realm of space, and finally the sunlight.*

René Girard makes quite similar statements in his reading of Shakespeare. In Shakespeare's plays a human universe has its end and its beginning in this erasing of differences. A new universe springs up from the resulting undifferentiation; the old one dissolves in it like a river in an ocean. By *universe* René Girard means differential system of culture. The Void, the undifferentiation, is also called the mimetic crisis. This is the ultimate social impasse, and is suddenly brought to an end by a violent event. Differences are reborn from contemplation of this violent and seemingly miraculous event.

Girard speaks of violent undifferentiation. The action described in the Hymn *Nāsadīya* seems to be violent as well. That action was done in someone's protection. *What stirred? Where? In whose protection?* In the beginning of the universe, then, there was destruction.

But where does this violent undifferentiation come from? How does it begin?

2. Desire came upon that one in the beginning ...

René Girard would find nothing surprising in that statement of the ancient *Rig Veda*. The violent undifferentiation, the violent Void, has its beginning in desire. Some questions arise, however. Whom did the desire come upon? How did it begin? In the beginning of what did it come? Did it come in the beginning of the creation? If so, what was created?

Girard might advise us to read Shakespeare to find the answers. Shakespearean characters suffer from desire. Desire strikes like lightning, and is as contagious as the plague.

3. Desire came upon that one ...

Upon whom did desire come? How did it begin?

How does it ever begin? It does not come upon one individual but simultaneously upon several. Desire is contagious; it spreads to others. Reading Shakespeare we can observe a repetition of the same desire suddenly striking close friends or brothers. How can we explain this strange property of desire?

An individual experiencing desire is called a subject of desire. However, desire has its source neither in him nor in the object of desire, but in the *mimetic relation the one has with the other*. The individual subject is a secondary reality. The more primary reality involves two people joined together by mimesis (imitation). This is the *primordial human relation*. The human ego has its beginning in its reflection in another's eyes. The *being* of the other is *a primordial divine*. It seems to have a divine value. And desire starts almost more with this transcendental admiration of the other's *being* than with the mimesis triggered thereby.

The wish to possess, customarily called *desire,* is then also a secondary reality. The subjective emotional experience of *thirst* for an object is just the visible part of what should be called desire. Desire should be understood as a process. It has its beginning, its middle, and its end. The process of desire is put in motion by mimesis. It develops because of mimesis; mimesis also will bring about its end. All this is *conflictual* mimesis, which implants conflict in human interactions, and ultimately ends in the violent undifferentiation of section 1.

4. Desire … was the first seed of mind

Reading Shakespeare we can trace desire from its beginning to its end. We can also trace its products. The process of desire can be triggered by mimesis among childhood friends or brothers. They form a unit, bound by the primordial mimetic relation. Growing up together they imitate each other's somehow random choices. They are encouraged to do so by their teachers, and by their friendship itself. Indeed, imitation is the very heart of friendship. It also binds society together. Society expects the development of desires. Girard assumes we do not know what we want. We have to learn our desires. Friends follow each other's choices, and create their *first shared divine image*. They persuade each other that an object is desirable by producing symbolic representations of its image as divine. Friends try to influence each other towards the same choice: they want to trigger mimesis. Mimesis is rewarding. The matching choice is a confirmation that the object is desirable.

In Shakespeare's plays, the dramatic chain of events usually starts with friends who mimetically create the shared divine image of an object that cannot be possessed by both at once. For example, Valentine and Proteus, the characters from *The Two Gentlemen of Verona*, mimetically create the image of Silvia as divine. Praising Silvia to Proteus, and inviting him to join in creating her image as divine, Valentine manages to provoke his friend to mimesis. He suffers from "bawd and cuckold" syndrome, Girard says. This is a widespread illness in Shakespeare. Proteus would eventually fall in love with Silvia. Valentine would become cuckolded. Proteus imitates Valentine's choice, as then does Valentine Proteus's. He inspires Proteus's choice so as to follow it himself and fall in love with the divine image of Silvia that he can now see in Proteus's eyes. The divinity of this image of the object of desire sets in motion the process of desire. It transforms Proteus and Valentine into the subjects of desire. Their previous unity breaks up into three separate elements: the two subjects before the same divine object of desire, and that object. These three constitute *the triangle of desire*.

The object and the subjects of desire acquire new lives of their own. The divine image sets all their minds in motion and starts to fill their psyches, motivating their behavior, and emboldening them to create a new external social reality. Desire is the process of creation and transformation of both human subjectivity and human interaction.

5. Poets seeking in their heart with wisdom found the bond of existence in non-existence

What energy is it, that may have put into the non-existence the bond of existence that the poets found there? We would say it is the *Desire* that *came ... in the beginning*. It does so by implanting a divine image of an *object* of desire into certain *subjects* of desire. The divine image of the object of desire puts in motion the process of transformation, which is pushed forward by mimesis. It injects a transforming force into the object and the subjects of desire. It is imitated by the object of desire who develops self-love. It changes former childhood friends into rivals. They will each continue to imitate the other in their desire for the object behind the divine image and in their attempts to overcome each other as rivals. They become model/obstacle/rival for each other. Girard calls relations of this sort *mimetic rivalry*. Such rivalry has no end. Not even winning can stop it, for that will only destroy the object of desire and the rivals themselves. The act of winning the object of desire will eradicate from its divine image its very divinity, thereby destroying the object of desire itself by removing the implanted model for its own self-love. Nor will winning stop the rivalry that has by now become the dominating model for interactions. Rivalry might well become the dominating model in the whole society. If it starts at the top of the society it can spread especially easily. It kills all a well-organized society's other models because they lose relevance to reality. Desire is then a process of transformation that ends with violent undifferentiation. Desire introduces into human relations a rivalry that ultimately becomes the dominating social model, and dissolves all cultural differences.

This violent undifferentiation is brought to an end by the isolated violent event that Girard calls *scapegoating*. Even this strange conclusion to the violence has its source in mimesis. Model images of enemies will proliferate. They will be imprinted in the heart of every individual. Ultimately each will choose to fight against the same enemy whose model has now successfully spread throughout the whole society. Killing this embodiment of the enemy's image will bring the war to the end. It will remove the pattern of rivalry from the society. The object perceived by all as a living model of the enemy will be killed. There will be no one else to fight with. The demon will be removed. Peace and order will be nearly at hand.

6. *Their* (the poets') *cord was extended across*

We have come as far as the violent undifferentiation and caught a glimpse of its resolution. Some questions arise at this point. Desire brings about both the creation and the destruction of the object and the subjects of desire. It starts with the mimetic creation of divine images. Surely, however, these are very minor gods at best. What relevance can they have to the beginning of the universe and its Creators? Are there any connections between the process of desire and the creation of the universe?

The Hymn *Nāsadīya* itself seems to ask this question.

(5) *Their* (the poets') *cord was extended across. Was there below? Was there above? There were seed-placers; there were powers. There was impulse beneath; there was giving-forth above.*

(6) *Who really knows? Who will here proclaim it? Whence was it produced? Whence is this creation? The gods came afterwards, with the creation of this universe. Who then knows whence it has arisen?*

Their cord was extended across, the *Rig Veda* says. Poets have their part in the creation of the universe by expressing in their language their understanding of the creation. This also is mimesis. Images, however, are not pure fantasy: they have their reference to reality. (3) *The life force*, say the poets of the Hymn, *was covered with emptiness.* The Poets too just arise from the emptiness by the power, perhaps, of heat; the beginning of the universe is a mystery also for them. They weave the world by focusing their attention on that mystery.

7. Whence is this creation? The gods came afterwards, with the creation of this universe

The Hymn *Nāsadīya* asks about the source of the creation, about the place from which it springs. *Whence is this creation?* It seems to be a little confused. It sees the creation as independent of the gods. *The gods came afterwards, with the creation of this universe.*

The Poets recognize that desire is the source of the creation. Desire *was the first seed of mind.* However, they do not understand how the universe was created, what the connection is between desire and the creation of the universe.

(6) *Who really knows? Who will here proclaim it? Whence was it produced? Whence is this creation?*

Creation has its source in the mimetic production of divine images having the power to produce human subjectivity and human behaviors. There is one divine image at the beginning of the process of desire, and another at the end. Desire starts with the divine image of the object of desire that triggers the process of desire. It ends with the divine image of the Creators of the universe and the sacrifice that triggers the creation of the universe.

What does really happen at the end of the process of desire? From the mystery of this end arises the creation of the universe. Without it that creation would be impossible. The mimetic explanation of how the violence of the endless revenge suddenly comes to an end, and peace emerges, we have already sketched in section 5. The Hymns, however, preferring a more transcendental explanation, attribute it to the action of the gods.

8. Violent undifferentiation and generative violence

The Hymn *Nāsadīya* meditates on the mystery of the creation of the new universe. It makes three strange findings, as section 1 has already pointed out. It connects the creation of the universe with desire; it separates creation from the gods and distinguishes it from the creation of the universe; it sees the life force as emerging from the violent undifferentiation. The Hymn *Nāsadīya* thus refers to two kinds of creation. One results from the process of desire in all its successive stages. The other has its beginning in the violent conclusion of that process. Each of these kinds of creation is triggered by a shared divine image and progresses by means of mimesis. For the first, the divine image is of the object of desire, while for the second it is the divine image of the Creator and the sacrifice. The violent undifferentiation is the last stage in the process of desire, where the first kind of creation has just been destroyed and the other is just about to begin. These two kinds of creation, triggered by two different divine images, are in opposition to each other; yet, at the same time, the second springs from the first.

The process of desire fills non-existence with the bond of existence, but, by providing a model for revenge and rivalry, it ends by destroying the existence it has created. A new universe emerges from the ruins of the existence desire built. The violent conclusion of the process of desire introduces the mechanism of scapegoating, which both ultimately brings to ruin the existence previously built by desire and, by providing new models for divine and sacrificial images, enables a new universe to emerge from those ruins. This universe is a world quite different from that built and destroyed by the process of desire. It is a world of normative order and *imperative* mimesis. Systems of norms emerge to prescribe proper objects of desire and proper actions for the various categories of people. These systems are built on the divine authority of both the Creator and the sacrifice, who reveal themselves at the climax of the violent undifferentiation.

Chapter II

*He to Whom the
Two Opposed Masses Looked
with Trembling in Their Hearts ...*

The Creator as Mediator of Desires

*He to whom the two opposed masses looked
with trembling in their hearts,
supported by his help, on whom
the rising sun shines down —
who is the god whom we should worship with the
oblation?*

The *Rig Veda*: *The Unknown God, The Golden Embryo*,
10.121, 6

The Hymn *The Unknown God, The Golden Embryo* develops an image of the Creator. Precisely in that development one sees the process Girard calls *victimage*, by means of which the shifting to the *imperative* mimesis is accomplished. The birth of the Creator then marks the completion of this shifting to the imperative mimesis. It is the Creator who has the power to change chaos into order, to produce the imperative mimesis. The Hymn *The Golden Embryo* explicates the circumstances surrounding the birth of the Creator, circumstances serving as clues that behind of the image of the Creator is the mimetic transformation of the original violent event into the sacrifice and the divine, transformation through which that violent event brings an end to the endless revenge. The Creator comes into being in the middle of a war between two opposed masses (the endless revenge). His coming unites them and brings an end to the war. He is not, however, born alone. The same watery womb, pregnant with the sacrifice, carries Dakṣa. What directly represents this original event is the image of Dakṣa. The Creator and the sacrifice are powerful transformed representations thereof.

1. The Creator as Mediator of Desires

The 10.121^{st} Hymn of the *Rig Veda, The Unknown God, The Golden Embryo,* describes the mystery itself of the creation of the universe, the transcendental experience of seeing and drawing the image of the Creator. With His birth the creation of the universe is set in motion.

The new universe begins where the process of desire finds its end. The lord of creation reveals himself to two polarized undifferentiated violent sides; presumably during a war: as the Hymn says, it is

(6) *He to whom the two opposed masses looked with trembling in their hearts.*

He is first seen during a *paroxysm of war* (Girard's term), the stage of the endless revenge sketched in chapter 1, section 5. He is seen simultaneously by both of the opposed masses. They share their feelings before him. Terrified by his powers and his grace, they look to him

(6) *with trembling in their hearts, supported by his help, on whom the rising sun shines down.*

By revealing himself, the lord of creation consolidates the opposed masses. They are united by seeing him simultaneously, and by sharing their feelings in front of him. He refocuses their shared desire for revenge. Nobody is angry with him; he is too powerful. The opposed masses shift their focus from their rival to him, the lord of creation. They want to worship him, to obey him. They want to learn: *Who is the god whom we should worship with the oblation?* They recognize him as the mediator of their desires:

(10) *O Prajāpati, lord of progeny, no one but you embraces all these creatures. Grant us the desires for which we offer you oblation. Let us be lords of riches.*

They no longer take it upon themselves to fulfill their desires. They delegate this fulfillment to the will of the god. An exchange with the god is established. Oblation is offered to the god in exchange for his granting them their desires.

This entire hymn thus contains all three crucial elements that Girard stresses in his explanation of mythical exegeses of creation. First, it is during a paroxysm of war, and to a people somehow already prepared to offer sacrifice, that the god first reveals himself. Second, by revealing himself, the god brings about a radical change in their feelings, for the opposed masses become united at seeing a new Other — Himself — whom they now adopt as their new mimetic Other. The whole rivalric mimetic relation disappears. Third, the people themselves were somehow ripe for his coming: they felt his powers; they saw him, as the Hymn *The Golden Embryo* says, *with trembling in their hearts*; they were ready to worship and to obey him.

2. Once he was born, he was the one lord of creation

With the phrase, *Once he was born*, the Hymn clearly signals that the one lord of creation was not just always there, but had his beginning in something other than himself: he had first to be born.

What, then, were the circumstances of his birth? How was he born?

He emerged from certain *high waters*:

(7) *When the high waters came, pregnant with the embryo that is everything, bringing forth fire, he arose from that as the one life's breath of the gods.*

These high waters, this flooding, can clearly be read as universal allusions to an all-encompassing undifferentiated chaos — perhaps even, in view of its *bringing forth fire* and of the violent chaos of *the two opposed masses*, to a Girardian "paroxysm of war." This violent undifferentiation, which the Hymn *Nāsadīya* seems to tell us already contains within itself the life force, was the medium from which he emerged — not directly, of course, but indirectly: out of the Golden Embryo.

The Hymn *The Golden Embryo* does not much discuss the origin of the Golden Embryo, saying only: (1) *In the beginning the Golden Embryo arose*; and, later, that (7) *the high waters* were *pregnant with* it. Still, we see that the life force hidden in the violent undifferentiation of the high waters formed itself into the Golden Embryo, and from this, in turn, the one lord of creation was born.

Not only the one lord of creation, however, was to be born at this moment, but also, and equally indirectly, the sacrifice. For the waters delivered not only the Golden Embryo, from which the one lord of creation was born, but also Dakṣa, who would be *bringing forth the sacrifice*:

(8) *He who in his greatness looked over the waters, which were pregnant with Dakṣa bringing forth the sacrifice, he who was the one god among all the gods ...*

Thus the sacrifice was not born directly from the waters, any more than was the one lord of creation. Rather, the life force hidden in the waters formed itself not only into the Golden Embryo, from which the one lord of creation arose, but also into Dakṣa, from whom the sacrifice was born. The one lord of creation could observe *the waters, which were pregnant with Dakṣa bringing forth the sacrifice.*

3. He who by his greatness became the one king of the world

What are the powers of the one lord of creation?

This powerful god came bearing peace. He transformed the chaos of war into the order of the new universe. He structured all of space.

(1) *He held in place the earth and this sky.*

It was

(5) *He by whom the awesome sky and the earth were made firm, by whom the dome of the sky was propped up, and the sun, who measured out the middle realm of space ...*

He is the center of the universe. His kingdom originates in his great powers, for it is

(3) *He who by his greatness became the one king of the world ...*

(4) *He who through his power owns these snowy mountains, and the ocean together with the river Rasā, they say; who has the quarters of the sky as his arms ...*

The Hymn *The Golden Embryo* speaks of this very powerful god, this one lord of creation, this issuer of commands and giver of life, quite simply as

(2) *He who gives life, who gives strength, whose command all the gods, his own, obey;*

adding that *his shadow is immortality — and death*, it describes him as

(8) *... the one god among all the gods.*

4. Chaos, destruction, creation, order

It may be worthwhile to recapitulate the central components of the discussion thus far, in preparation for a mimetic analysis of them. It is chaos and destruction, expressed by the metaphor of the high waters, in the midst of which, before the two opposed masses, the creation of the universe began. Chaos and destruction were the womb from which the lord of creation was born. Chaos it is, also, that the lord of creation has the power to transform into universal order. But the same chaos, the same high waters, from which the lord of creation emerged, were also bringing forth the mysterious Dakṣa, from whom in turn sacrifice would be born.

The same waters that brought forth the Golden
Embryo were pregnant with Dakṣa. Both the one
lord of creation and the sacrifice thus have their
beginning inside the same womb. The sacrifice,
however, is not born directly from the waters. It
is born from Dakṣa. Only Dakṣa emerged
directly from the water. Likewise the one lord of
creation was born from the Golden Embryo. This
curious indirection with regard to the births of
the sacrifice and of the god is extremely
significant from the Girardian point of view. In
this view, both of them would be transformed
representations of the original violent event.
Only the image of Dakṣa seems to represent the
reality of that original event.

There are both mimetic and transcendental
explanations of the beginning of the universe.
The transcendental one is a crucial part of the
creation itself. It incorporates into the creation
the concepts of the sacrifice and the Creator. The
mimetic one deals with the question mimetic
theory would ask, not about first causes, nor
about a historical sequence of events, but the
question: What was the model for this
beginning? The Creator and the sacrifice are the
transformed divine images of something real,
Girard would claim, images that become
extremely powerful if implanted into many
individuals. The sacrifice represents the means of
transforming violence into peace. The Creator
represents a vehicle for the fulfillment of human
desires.

What, then, is the reality of which both images
are images? It is the reality of the founding

murder, Girard would claim. This is one of the *Things Hidden since the Foundation of the World* described by Girard in his book with that title. We can infer this reality both from the transformed religious images and from the mimetic logic of the process of desire. In the images of the Creator and the sacrifice we can see what today we would call scapegoating, which we try to expose and condemn. *Scapegoat* is the term for a victim, falsely blamed for bringing chaos, whose death is falsely perceived as restoring order. This victim might be represented by sacred images, be they demonic or divine. The Creator is the consecrated image of such a victim. Sacrifice is the consecrated image of this scapegoating. The reality of the founding murder, however, can also be inferred from the mimetic logic of the process of desire, according to which the endless cycle of revenge spurred by imitation of revenge finally does end when the model of revenge is removed from society. This removal is ultimately achieved by the polarization of the whole society against an individual victim, who is perceived as an embodiment of the model enemy. The collective killing of this scapegoat brings the peace. This scapegoat is everyone's one last rival. As if with one mind, the people are united in their violent action against this one person. Once he is killed, the war stops because there is no rival left. And this demonized scapegoat then provides a model for the images of the Creator and the sacrifice.

Girard assumes that the original violent scapegoating is real. It has its roots in the process of desire, of which it is the logical conclusion. The Creator and the sacrifice are the lingering images of this scapegoating. They emerge simultaneously in the individual minds of people unanimously united against the demonic scapegoat. Far from being purely imaginary, these images are the transformed memory of a real scapegoating. Being shared by so many people, they become a crucial part of the creation of the new universe: indeed, they become its very foundation. They have the power to produce the imperative mimesis. Scapegoating is almost completely deconstructed today, but it still exists as a reality of human interaction. It has its roots in conflictual mimesis and has a mimetic explanation.

The mimetic explanation of scapegoating, however, is powerless by itself to create a new universe. Nor is the original scapegoating usually directly described by most religious narratives, so successfully is it transformed into the ritual of sacrifice, and the Creator. The Hymn of *The Golden Embryo*, however, with its idea of Dakṣa, provides a quite complex picture of the original scapegoating. In Dakṣa himself we see evidence both of the scapegoating and of its transformation into sacrifice. Thus, the Hymn of *The Golden Embryo* would appear to be the exposition of a metaphysics so comprehensive as to be revealing its own mimetic sources.

Chapter III

With the Sacrifice the Gods Sacrificed to the Sacrifice

The Violence at the Beginning of the World

With the sacrifice
the gods sacrificed to the sacrifice.
These were the first ritual laws.
These very powers reached the dome of sky
where dwell the Sādhyas, the ancient gods.

The *Rig Veda: Puruṣa-Sūkta*, or *The Hymn of Man*, 10.90, 16

The *Hymn of Man* describes directly what the Hymn *The Golden Embryo* only provided circumstantial evidence for: the original scapegoating is transformed into the founding murder for the new universe by providing a model for the ritual of sacrifice and divinity. This is precisely what ties the process of desire to the creation of the new universe. The scapegoating by which the process of desire is concluded constitutes the beginning of the new universe.

The Man of this Hymn, like the Dakḷa of the Hymn of *The Golden Embryo,* serves as another representation of the reality of scape-goating. In this Hymn one can see the mimetic transformation of the Man — the scapegoat — into divinity, and of his dismembering — his scapegoating — into the ritual of sacrifice, which, taken together, provide the foundation for the new universe. What explains the effectiveness of the ritual of sacrifice as a mechanism for changing chaos into order is *imperative* mimesis.

1. The founding murder and its copy

In the line

(16) *With the sacrifice the gods sacrificed to the sacrifice,*

Wendy Doniger O'Flaherty, the translator of these hymns, must have found the hypnotic three-fold repetition of the vocable "sacrifice" too mesmerizingly puzzling for the Western reader, for she confirms, "The meaning is that Puruṣa (the Man) was both the victim that the gods sacrificed and the divinity to whom the sacrifice was dedicated." Perhaps thinking that still sounds too strange, she reiterates: "that is, he was both the subject and the object of the sacrifice." But exactly this idea, that the subject and the object — the sacrificial victim, and the divinity to whom the sacrifice is dedicated — should be identical, lies at the heart of the Girardian concept of the founding murder. Both victim and divinity represent the same scapegoating, which they transform into the founding murder by their very merging. In *The Hymn of Man* the notion of the founding murder seems to underlie the text itself. The ritual of sacrifice and the divinity are presented as emerging from the dismembered Man. Like Dakṣa, the Man represents the scapegoating from which the sacrifice is born. So clearly and directly does its author, presumably a believer in the divinity of the ritual of sacrifice, see and describe the Man, the sacrifice, the divinity, and the transformation of the image of the Man, that, almost inadvertently, the Hymn also divulges the mimetic explanation of the origin of these divine images.

In *The Hymn of Man* the transformation of the scapegoating into the ritual of sacrifice is not yet completed. *The Hymn* of *Man* cannot free itself from the ambiguity inherent in the process of making copies. We can observe mimesis at work. The original victim (the Man) multiplies into copies. The ritual of the sacrifice is first carried out by the gods, who take as their authority for doing so their understanding of the wishes of the Man himself. Doing what the Man expects to be done is the first model of *imperative* mimesis.

When the gods carried out the first ritual of the sacrifice, the receiver of the sacrifice still too closely resembles the sacrifice itself. At the same time he is somewhat different, because he is already divine. The original victim (the model) and the act of sacrifice and the divinity (the copies) are not well differentiated in the mind of the poet, nor are they entirely identical. They are at once different and the same.

The language of *The Hymn of Man* reflects a memory of the empirical reality, a memory fresh enough in the poet's mind to nourish the ambiguity. Certainly contemporary readers of the ancient text cannot share the same ambiguity. We cannot help but distinguish between the victim and the divinity, between the divinity and the sacrificial offering. These are separate constructs in our language, for we have lost all recollection of the original. For us the transformation of the scapegoating into the sacrificial ritual and the divinity has been completed.

2. These were the first ritual laws

The Hymn of Man describes the emerging of the first ritual laws, whose source is in the transformation of the scapegoating into the ritual of sacrifice. This transformation is accomplished by the gods, for they are first sacrificers, and thereby set an example of proper action:

(16) *The gods sacrificed to the sacrifice. These were the first ritual laws.*

In framing the ritual of the sacrifice the gods take as their authority the example of what the Man did to himself. They just repeat what the Man did, and they do so for Him. They provide the perfect model of how to follow the Man's example in making offering to Him. Thereafter, making offering to the Man is taken for granted, and has its rationale in the example set by the gods.

The gods made such sacrifice the obligatory way of transforming chaos into order. They show exactly what should be done to get the desired effects. Dismemberment of the Man is the first recipe for the desired effects. Any causal connection linking repetition of this action to the desired effects, however, seems so unpredictable as to require the mediation of the gods or their representatives for its success. They become the legitimate sources of the authoritative knowledge as to what behavior is appropriate. They acquire the authority to formulate the relevant laws. This transformation of the original dismembering into the ritual of sacrifice is the beginning of the imperative order, and of the imperative mimesis which demands imitative repetition of the patterns laid down by a recognized authority.

3. From the sacrifice in which everything was offered, the melted fat was collected

The ritual of sacrifice is perceived as the source of the matter (the *melted fat*) from which to shape living beings. *The Hymn of Man* treats literally what today would be a metaphor for the shaping of cultural meaning by means of *imperative* mimesis. The creative power of the remains of the ritual of sacrifice stems from the fact that the sacrifice is a copy of the dismembering of the Man. The ritual killing of a sacrificial victim and the sacrificial offering itself are duplicates of the Man, the original victim. The mysterious authority of the original is projected on the copies. In the course of the sacrifice *everything was offered* (8, 9). Nothing, presumably, was withheld or saved aside. The only remains were the *melted fat*. This *was collected and he* — who, we would wonder, is this *he*? — *made it into those beasts who live in the air, in the forest, and in villages* (8). Who is this *he* who shapes living beings? Does *he* refer to the original Man, or to one of his ritualistic copies? In fact *he* seems to refer to all of these in one. For the Man shaped everything once, using his own sacrificial remains. And he did it again, now using the gods as intermediaries. And, in future mimetic repetition, he will do so yet again, and again.

The remains of the sacrifice are the matter to produce, to transform — in short, to shape — human culture. From them are born the sacred language, the sacred music, the prayers:

(9) *From that sacrifice in which everything was offered, the verses and chants were born, the metres were born from it, and from it the formulas were born.*

Common animals spring from the sacrifice:

(10) Horses were born from it, and those other animals that have two rows of teeth; cows were born from it, and from it goats and sheep were born.

Notice, however, that it is only domestic animals, not wild ones, that *The Hymn of Man* catalogues, and most of these are, in fact, potentially sacrificial (Girard would maintain that this focus simply confirms that domestication itself arose from sacrifice, or rather, from its requirement of a steady supply of victims). Even social stratification receives its shape from the remains of the sacrificial Man's body parts:

(11) When they divided the Man, into how many parts did they apportion him? What do they call his mouth, his two arms and thighs and feet?

(12) His mouth became the Brahmin; his arms were made into the Warrior, his thighs the People, and from his feet the Servants were born.

Using the Man's body parts the gods also organized space, or, as the Hymn of Man has it, *set the worlds in order*:

(13) The moon was born from his mind; from his eye the sun was born. Indra and Agni came from his mouth, and from his vital breath the Wind was born.

(14) From his navel the middle realm of space arose; from his head the sky evolved. From his two feet came the earth, and the

quarters of the sky from his ear. Thus they set the worlds in order.

The matter provided by the sacrifice shapes every aspect of culture. The seemingly strange view, held by *The Hymn of Man*, that sacrifice is the source of human culture, is one Girard treats quite seriously. Sacrifice really is a machine that transforms chaos into culture by virtue of its power to generate imperative mimesis. This machine is driven by widespread belief in the scapegoat and in his miraculous power to change the inescapable war of endless revenge into a new order. Girard finds this strange power inherent in all such *generative violence. The Hymn of Man* draws a picture of the transforming powers of the generative violence of sacrifice. Is it also aware of where these powers come from?

4. The Man, the sacrifice born at the beginning

The universe was created because the gods introduced the ritual of sacrifice and dedicated it to the Man. The generative powers of the ritual of sacrifice come from the mimetic connection of that ritual with the Man. It is not the Man himself, however, but his copies, who have these creative powers. *The Hymn of Man* develops two independent ways to describe the original scapegoating that concluded the process of desire. Like Dakṣa, the Man represents both the reality of that original scapegoating and its transformation into the divine ritual of sacrifice, which, in turn, represents the result of this transformation. Such transformed images have the power to shape living beings. They hold within themselves an ability to organize people's actions and to mediate their desires.

The language of *The Hymn of Man* distinguishes between the Man and the matter shaping the universe. The Man provides the matter so long as he is transformed into the sacrifice and the divine. That matter is described as the remains of the sacrifice: the melted fat. It is also named Virāj (or later, Prakṛti). The Man is different from Virāj, though each comes from the other:

(5) *From him Virāj was born, and from Virāj came the Man.*

We can interpret that last line as follows: the Man gives birth to Virāj because the Man is copied by the ritual of the sacrifice which is the source of Virāj. It is Virāj, in turn, from whom the Man comes, because the sacrifice, which provides the divine matter, transforms the Man into divinity. The transformation of the Man into the sacrifice must continually be repeated if it is to provide the divine matter. The divinity of the matter, in turn, becomes projected on the Man and on his transformation into the sacrifice. The Man's divine power comes from his ability to provide the model for the sacrifice. The power of the copy, in turn, depends on maintaining the Man's ability to provide the model. In this way the relation between the Man (later called

Puruṣa) and the matter (later called Prakṛti) can be interpreted as the mimetic relation between the original scapegoat and its sacrificial copy, the latter having the character of a machine for producing the matter that will shape the universe.

The Hymn of Man captures the mimetic relation between the original violent scapegoating and its transformed copy. This mimetic relation connects the end of the sort of existence produced by the process of desire with the beginning of the new universe. Mimesis changes the original scapegoating into the founding murder of the new universe. The Man is the original scapegoat, but the Man is also the later sacrifice. The notions of scapegoat and of sacrifice are similar but not identical. The sacrifice has generative powers of its own; so has the Man. However the Man, the original scapegoat, acquires his powers from his transformation into the sacrifice. He is *whatever has been and whatever is to be*, all owing to this transformation. More than just the beginning of the universe, he is also its middle and its end.

5. The Man is yet more than this. All creatures are a quarter of him; three quarters are what is immortal in heaven

While praising the Man, *The Hymn of Man* also describes the Man's transformation into divinity, and the dependence of this transformation on mankind's belief in the power of sacrifice.

(1) *The Man has a thousand heads, a thousand eyes, a thousand feet. He pervaded the earth on all sides and extended beyond it as far as ten fingers.*

(2) *It is the Man who is all this, whatever has been and whatever is to be. He is the ruler of immortality, when he grows beyond everything through food.*

(3) *Such is his greatness, and the Man is yet more than this. All creatures are a quarter of him; three quarters are what is immortal in heaven.*

Much the larger part of the Man is what is divine (*immortal*). The Man is also the ruler of the divine. This power of the Man, however, is presented by the Hymn as conditional: *He is the ruler of immortality, when he grows beyond everything through food.* Wendy Doniger, the translator, comments that "food" here surely refers to the sacrificial offering. Thus the Man only grows into the ruler of the divine (*ruler of immortality*) through the offerings that mankind's belief in the divinity of sacrifice motivates.

The Hymn of Man points out yet another aspect of the Man's greatness. One full quarter of the Man remains on the earth, transformed into creatures. This quarter, moreover, seems to be crucial for his transformation into divinity.

(4) *With three quarters the Man rose upwards, and one quarter of him still remains here. From this he spread out in all*

directions, into that which eats and that which does not eat.

Later this image of the Man will develop into the *Mahābhārata*'s image of Kṛṣṇa, that avatar of the God Viṣṇu, in the context of the endless war of Kurukṣetra. Kṛṣṇa there is a man who will die as a human, but he is also the god who demands sacrifice from other humans. The human part of the dead Kṛṣṇa will remain on this earth. The Man's greatness likewise depends on his death as a human. The image of this death is represented by the ritual of sacrifice. This is the death of the scapegoat. Once again we see how the seeming paradoxes, in terms of which the poetic language of this Hymn describes the image of the Man, may be taken as describing the mimetic transformation of scapegoat and scapegoating into divinity and the ritual of sacrifice.

Chapter IV

What Was the Original Model, and What Was the Copy ...?

On Generative Violence

What was the original model,
and what was the copy,
and what was the connection between them?
What was the butter, ... ,
what was the invocation, and the chant,
when all the gods sacrificed the god?

The *Rig Veda: The Creation of the Sacrifice*, 10.130, 3

> The sacrifice as woven by the sages is perceived here as highly mimetic. It harmonizes with the models provided by the primeval sacrifice and the Man. The poet's concern about the mimetic details signals awareness that the copy should perfectly match the original to allow the shift to the imperative mimesis to continue.

1. On making sacrificial copies

The poet,

> (6) *with the eye that is mind, in thought ... sees those who were the first to offer this sacrifice.*

And yet he is puzzled; he sees something beyond them. He sees their action as that of making a copy. The poet, as if with blurred vision, wonders:

> (3) *What was the original model, and what was the copy, and what was the connection between them?*

He seems to be unable to distinguish between *the primeval sacrifice* (6) and the original scapegoating it copies. The action of the gods when they *all ... sacrificed the god* was surely mimetic. The poet, however, wants to know the exact details:

> (3) *What was the butter, and what the enclosing wood? What was the metre, what was the invocation, and the chant, when all the gods sacrificed the god?*

2. The seven divine sages harmonized with the original models

The poet also sees the human sages, the founding fathers. He perceives their action of sacrifice too as mimetic. However, their action is not just a simple imitation of the gods.

(7) *The seven divine sages harmonized with the original models.*

The poet uses the grammatical plural here: *models.* He refers both to the model provided when *all the gods sacrificed the god,* and to the supposed original that was the model for the gods as well. The original is not directly known; it is not even imaginable. Yet, the founding fathers, the seven sages, harmonized mimetically with everything they could; with the model provided by the gods, and with the original model provided to the gods:

(7) *The ritual repetitions harmonized with the chants and with the metres.*

The ritual repetitions harmonized with the model provided by the gods. However,

(7) *the seven divine sages harmonized with the original models.*

The sages' vision reached beyond the action of the gods. The founding fathers, the sages, did not simply imitate the action of the gods. They harmonized with the model provided by the gods and with the original as well. They participated in the creation of the sacrifice by harmonizing with the models.

3. Seeing with the eye that is mind

The poet uses the metaphor of weaving to describe the sacrifice.

(1) *The sacrifice ... is spread out with threads on all sides.*

It is the Man (see *The Hymn of Man*) who

(2) *has spread it out upon this dome of the sky.*

It is also he who

(2) *stretches the warp and draws the weft.*

Without the Man, the weaving of the sacrifice would be impossible. The sacrifice

(1) *is woven by these fathers,*

(6) *the human sages.*

(1) *They sit by the loom that is stretched tight.*

The sacrifice is

(1) *drawn tight with a hundred and one divine acts.*

The sages weave the sacrifice as, with their mystical vision, they approach (come near) the original model.

(1) *The sacrifice ... is woven by these fathers as they come near: "Weave forward, weave backward," they say as they sit by the loom that is stretched tight.*

The Man provides the base for weaving the fabric, and the divine acts keep the threads tight. The sages weave the sacrifice in cooperation with the Man. It was the Man who spread the sacrifice out. However, the primeval ritual of the sacrifice was conducted by the gods. The poet asks,

(3) *when all the gods sacrificed the god ... what was the original model, and what was the copy and what was the connection between them?*

The primeval sacrifice conducted by the gods was the model for the sages. The poet can see it *with the eye that is mind.* But

(6) *the primeval sacrifice was born.*

Behind the sacrifice conducted by the gods is the Man. The sages just follow the gods in repeating the ritual. They cooperate also with the Man in their weaving of the sacrifice. The poet sees all of this. He sees those who were the first to offer the sacrifice. Looking back

(7) *along the path of those who went before*

gives the wise men the power and the vision to know what must be done, and how.

The poet differentiates himself from the subject he tries to describe. Seeing *with the eye that is mind* (6), he tries to describe the empirical reality of the sacrifice — its beginning and development. He is much closer to that reality than we are. He still can see what we cannot. He sees mimetic repetition — Girardian *doubling* — when he looks at this. He sees a model and its copy. *The Creation of the Sacrifice* is almost a Hymn in praise of (imperative) Mimesis.

Conclusions

In my rereading of the Creation Hymns of the *Rig Veda* I have been tracing *mimesis*. I have found *conflictual* mimesis in the Hymn *Nāsadīya*. *The Hymn of Man* and *The Golden Embryo*, in turn, refer to the mimetic production of the divine image of the Creator and the sacrifice. They capture the process of shifting to the *imperative* mimesis. The Hymn *The Creation of the Sacrifice* is concerned with the imperative mimesis of the mimetic repetition of the ritual of the sacrifice.

The Hymn *Nāsadīya* makes a connection between the creation and desire. Desire is able to put into the non-existence the bond of existence. The process of desire, however, is self-destructive. It implants a permanent conflict into human interaction and ultimately destroys the existence it has produced. The process of desire is governed by conflictual mimesis. The Hymn *Nāsadīya* also makes a connection between the Void that was in the beginning and the life force that Void contains. The Void can be understood as the violent undifferentiation, a Girardian term referring to the last stage of the process of desire. This is the stage of endless revenge. The war of revenge is brought to an end by a violent event, which is the killing of a person who seems to be

53

each individual's personal enemy. This killing is the original scapegoating. Peace and the creation of the new universe seem to be triggered by this event, which provides the model for the mimetic creation of the divine images of the Creator and of the sacrifice.

The Hymn *The Golden Embryo* describes the emerging of the Creator in the middle of the war and its violent undifferentiation. The same womb of violent undifferentiation was carrying Dakşa pregnant with the sacrifice. *The Hymn of Man* focuses on the mimetic production of the divine images of the Creator and the sacrifice by making copies of the original violent event. The Hymn *The Creation of the Sacrifice* points out the importance of the role the process of making copies plays in recreating the ritual of sacrifice.

Appendix

Creation Hymns of the Rig Veda
(in the Wendy Doniger translation)

10.129 Creation Hymn (*Nāsadīya*)

1. There was neither non-existence nor existence then; there was neither the realm of space nor the sky which is beyond. What stirred? Where? In whose protection? Was there water, bottomlessly deep?

2. There was neither death nor immortality then. There was no distinguishing sign of night nor of day. That one breathed, windless, by its own impulse. Other than that there was nothing beyond.

3. Darkness was hidden by darkness in the beginning; with no distinguishing sign, all this was water. The life force that was covered with emptiness, that one arose though the power of heat.

4. Desire came upon that one in the beginning; that was the first seed of mind. Poets seeking in their heart with wisdom found the bond of existence in non-existence.

5. Their cord was extended across. Was there below?
Was there above? There were seed-placers; there
were powers. There was impulse beneath; there
was giving-forth above.

6. Who really knows? Who will here proclaim it?
Whence was it produced? Whence is this creation?
The gods came afterwards, with the creation of this
universe. Who then knows whence it has arisen?

7. Whence this creation has arisen — perhaps it
formed itself, or perhaps it did not — the one who
looks down on it, in the highest heaven, only he
knows — or perhaps he does not know.

10.121 The Unknown God, the Golden Embryo

1. In the beginning the Golden Embryo arose. Once he was born, he was the one lord of creation. He held in place the earth and this sky. Who is the god whom we should worship with the oblation?

2. He who gives life, who gives strength, whose command all the gods, his own, obey; his shadow is immortality — and death. Who is the god whom we should worship with the oblation?

3. He who by his greatness became the one king of the world that breathes and blinks, who rules over his two-footed and four-footed creatures — who is the god whom we should worship with the oblation?

4. He who through his power owns these snowy mountains, and the ocean together with the river Rasā, they say; who has the quarters of the sky as his two arms — who is the god whom we should worship with the oblation?

5. He by whom the awesome sky and the earth were made firm, by whom the dome of the sky was propped up, and the sun, who measured out the middle realm of space — who is the god whom we should worship with the oblation?

6. He to whom the two opposed masses looked with trembling in their hearts, supported by his help, on whom the rising sun shines down — who is the god whom we should worship with the oblation?

7. When the high waters came, pregnant with the embryo that is everything, bringing forth fire, he arose from that as the one life's breath of the gods. Who is the god whom we should worship with the oblation?

8. He who in his greatness looked over the waters, which were pregnant with Dakṣa, bringing forth the sacrifice, he who was the one god among all the gods — who is the god whom we should worship with the oblation?

9. Let him not harm us, he who fathered the earth and created the sky, whose laws are true, who created the high, shining waters. Who is the god whom we should worship with the oblation?

10. O Prajāpati, lord of progeny, no one but you embraces all these creatures. Grant us the desires for which we offer you oblation. Let us be lords of riches.

10.90 *Puruṣa-Sūkta*, or The Hymn of Man

1. The Man has a thousand heads, a thousand eyes, a thousand feet. He pervaded the earth on all sides and extended beyond it as far as ten fingers.

2. It is the Man who is all this, whatever has been and whatever is to be. He is the ruler of immortality, when he grows beyond everything through food.

3. Such is his greatness, and the Man is yet more than this. All creatures are a quarter of him; three quarters are what is immortal in heaven.

4. With three quarters the Man rose upwards, and one quarter of him still remains here. From this he spread out in all directions, into that which eats and that which does not eat.

5. From him Virāj was born, and from Virāj came the Man. When he was born, he ranged beyond the earth behind and before.

6. When the gods spread the sacrifice with the Man as the offering, spring was the clarified butter, summer the fuel, autumn the oblation.

7. They anointed the Man, the sacrifice born at the beginning, upon the sacred grass. With him the gods, Sādhyas, and sages sacrificed.

8. From that sacrifice in which everything was offered, the melted fat was collected, and he made it into those beasts who live in the air, in the forest, and in villages.

9. From that sacrifice in which everything was offered, the verses and chants were born, the metres were born from it, and from it the formulas were born.

10. Horses were born from it, and those other animals that have two rows of teeth; cows were born from it, and from it goats and sheep were born.

11. When they divided the Man, into how many parts did they apportion him? What do they call his mouth, his two arms and thighs and feet?

12. His mouth became the Brahmin; his arms were made into the Warrior, his thighs the People, and from his feet the Servants were born.

13. The moon was born from his mind; from his eye the sun was born. Indra and Agni came from his mouth, and from his vital breath the Wind was born.

14. From his navel the middle realm of space arose; from his head the sky evolved. From his two feet came the earth, and the quarters of the sky from his ear. Thus they set the worlds in order.

15. There were seven enclosing-sticks for him, and thrice seven fuel-sticks, when the gods, spreading the sacrifice, bound the Man as the sacrificial beast.

16. With the sacrifice the gods sacrificed to the sacrifice. These were the first ritual laws. These very powers reached the dome of the sky where dwell the Sādhyas, the ancient gods.

10.130 The Creation of the Sacrifice

1. The sacrifice that is spread out with threads on all sides, drawn tight with a hundred and one divine acts, is woven by these fathers as they come near: "Weave forward, weave backward," they say as they sit by the loom that is stretched tight.

2. The Man stretches the warp and draws the weft; the Man has spread it out upon this dome of the sky. These are the pegs, that are fastened in place; they made the melodies into the shuttles for weaving.

3. What was the original model, and what was the copy, and what was the connection between them? What was the butter, and what the enclosing wood? What was the metre, what was the invocation, and the chant, when all the gods sacrificed the god?

4. The Gāyatrī metre was the yoke-mate of Agni; Savitṛ joined with the Uṣṇi metre, and with the Anuṣṭubh metre was Soma that reverberates with the chants. The Bṛhatī metre resonated in the voice of Bṛhaspati.

5. The Virāj metre was the privilege of Mitra and Varuṇa; the Triṣṭubh metre was part of the day of Indra. The Jagatī entered into all the gods. That was the model for the human sages.

6. That was the model for the human sages, our fathers, when the primeval sacrifice was born. With the eye that is mind, in thought I see those who were the first to offer this sacrifice.

7. The ritual repetitions harmonized with the chants and with the metres; the seven divine sages harmonized with the original models. When the wise men looked back along the path of those who went before, they took up the reins like charioteers.

More TLVP offerings by B. Mikolajewska

"Good" Violence Versus "Bad": A Girardian Analysis of
King Janamejaya's Snake Sacrifice and Allied Events
ISBN-10: 1-929865-29-5

The *Live Art* Series

Child's Play
ISBN-10: 1-929865-06-6

The Witches of the Harz
ISBN-10: 1-929865-11-2

This Is Us

Vol. 1: Doing Math — Category Theorists at Buffalo
ISBN-10: 0-9659529-7-5 (full color)
ISBN-10: 0-9659529-3-2 (grey-scale)

Vol. 2: Symposium — Celebrating ∧ ^with^ ∧ Saunders
ISBN-10: 1-929865-01-5

Vol. 3: Facing Off
ISBN-10: 1-929865-00-7

The Adventures of Marysia — Przygodi Marysi

Part 1: At the Playground
ISBN-10: 1-929865-08-2

Part 2: Going Out for Ice Cream
ISBN-10: 1-929865-09-0

Inne książki Barbary Mikołajewskiej

Zjawisko Wspólnoty
ISBN-10: 0-9659529-2-4

Na początku na to jedno przyszło pożądanie ... :
Hymny *Rigwedy* o stworzeniu świata
ISBN-10: 1-929865-25-2

Barbara Mikołajewska opowiada *Mahabharatę*

Księgi I-II – Adi Parva & Sabha Parva
ISBN-10: 1-929865-34-1

Księga III – Vana Parva
ISBN-10: 1-929865-35-X

Księgi IV-V – Virata Parva & Udyoga Parva
ISBN-10: 1-929865-36-8

Księgi VI-VII – Bhiszma Parva & Drona Parva
ISBN-10: 1-929865-37-6

Księgi VIII-XI – Karna Parva, Śalja Parva, Sauptika
Parva & Stree Parva
ISBN-10: 1-929865-38-4

Księga XII, cz. I – Santi Parva
ISBN-10: 1-929865-39-2